James
Madison

By United Library

https://campsite.bio/unitedlibrary

Table of Contents

Introduction

Do you want to learn about James Madison?

James Madison was America's first politician. He was a Founding Father, the fourth President of the United States, and an oligarch. This book tells his story.

James Madison was one of America's Founding Fathers, and he played an essential role in the early years of the nation. Born in Virginia in 1751, Madison attended the College of New Jersey (now Princeton University) before returning to Virginia to study law. He quickly rose to prominence in Virginia politics, and he was a key figure in the movement for independence from Britain. After the war, Madison played a leading role in drafting the Constitution and helped to ratify it through his work on the Federalist Papers.

Madison then served as a member of the House of Representatives and as Secretary of State under President Thomas Jefferson. In 1809, Madison was elected as the fourth President of the United States. He is best known for his leadership during the War of 1812, and for his later work as a founding member of the Democratic Party. Throughout his career, Madison always advocated for a strong federal government, and he is considered one of the most important political thinkers in American history.

You will learn about Madison's life as a Founding Father, President, and Oligarch in this biography. It is packed with information that will help you understand one of the most important figures in American history.

James Madison

James Madison (March 16, 1751-June 28, 1836) was an American politician and political theorist. He was the fourth president of the United States from 1809 to 1817. He is considered one of the most influential "Founding Fathers of the United States" for his contribution to the drafting of the U.S. Constitution and the U.S. Bill of Rights, to the point of being nicknamed "The Father of the Constitution."

Madison inherited his estate, Montpelier, in Virginia, and owned hundreds of slaves. He served as a member of the Virginia House of Delegates and as a member of the Continental Congress prior to the introduction of the U.S. Constitution. After the Philadelphia Convention, Madison was one of the people who led the movement to pass the new constitution both nationally and in Virginia. His collaboration with Alexander Hamilton and John Jay produced the essays known as *The Federalist* Papers, articles considered to be the main basis on which the U.S. Constitution was ratified. Madison changed his mind about his personal politics. At first he believed that a strong central government would be best, but eventually he came to support the idea that the states should have more power than the central government. At the end of his life he came to accept a balanced idea in which the states and the federal government share power equally.

In 1789, Madison became a leader in the U.S. House of Representatives in which he wrote many fundamental laws. He is recognized as the writer of the first 10 amendments to the U.S. Constitution, which became known as the Bill of Rights. He worked closely with the new President George Washington in organizing the new federal government. Breaking ties with Hamilton and the Federalist Party in 1791, he and Thomas Jefferson organized the Democratic-Republican Party. In response to the Alien and Sedition Acts Jefferson and Madison wrote the Virginia and Kentucky Resolutions, arguing that the states had the power to nullify laws as unconstitutional.

Serving as Jefferson's secretary of state, Madison oversaw the Louisiana Purchase, which doubled the size of the country. Madison became president after Jefferson and was reelected in 1813. His presidency brought prosperity that lasted for several years. After a series of diplomatic protests and a trade Embargo against the United Kingdom, he led the United States into the Anglo-American War of 1812. The war was a disastrous decision, as the country had neither a strong military nor a powerful financial system. In addition, the country did not have a central bank, something Madison opposed throughout his life.

Early years and education

James Madison Jr. was born on the Belle Grove estate near Port Conway, Virginia on March 16, 1751, where his mother had returned to give birth. He became the firstborn of 12 children. His parents, James Madison Sr. and Nelly Madison, had seven other sons and four daughters. Three of these sons died in infancy, including one who was stillborn. In the summer of 1775, his sister Elizabeth at age 7 and his brother Reuben at age 3 died during an epidemic of dysentery that struck the county due to water contamination.

His father, James Madison Sr. (1723-1801), was a tobacco planter who had grown up on the family estate, then known as Pleasurable Mount in Orange County, Virginia. He came to inherit the property as an adult. Later he acquired more property as well as more slaves. Owning 5,000 acres (20.23 km²), he was the largest landowner in the entire county. James' mother, Nelly Conway Madison, (1731-1829) was born in Port Conway, the daughter of a tobacco planter and merchant. James and Nelly were married on September 15, 1749. In those years, the southern colonies of the United States were in the process of becoming slave-based societies, a society in which the economy became completely dependent on slavery and landed masters formed the political prominence.

From the ages of 11 to 16, little "Jemmy" Madison was sent to study with Donald Robertson, a teacher on the Innes estate in King and Queen County, in the Tidewater region. Robertson was a Scottish schoolmaster, who served as a tutor to the children of prominent families in the area. Under Robertson, Madison learned mathematics, geography, and classical and modern languages. He credited Robertson with instilling in him his desire for learning.

At the age of 16 she returned to Montpelier where she began a two-year course with Reverend Thomas Martin to prepare for college. In contrast to many college-seeking young men, Madison did not decide to attend the College of William and Mary because the climate of Williamsburg (Virginia) would have affected his failing health. Instead, in 1769 he decided to attend the College of New Jersey, now known as Princeton University, where he met and befriended Philip Freneau, a famous poet. Madison proposed marriage to Freneau's sister, Mary, but she turned him down.

Although his long hours of work and intellectual concentration took a toll on his health, Madison graduated in 1771. His studies included Latin, ancient Greek, the natural sciences, geography, mathematics, rhetoric, and philosophy. Great emphasis was given to rhetoric and debate. Madison helped found the American Whig society to compete directly with his classmate Aaron Burr's Cliosophical society. After graduating, Madison remained at Princeton to learn Hebrew and political philosophy under the university's president, John Witherspoon, before returning to Montpelier in the spring of 1772. He became fluent in Hebrew. Madison studied law out of personal interest in public policy, not because he intended to practice law.

At just 1.63 cm (5'4") tall, he is the shortest U.S. president to ever serve in office.

Religion

Although educated by a Presbyterian minister, Madison was an avid reader of deistic tracts. In his adult life, Madison paid no attention to religion. Biographer Hutson notes that after his college life, historians find no clue as to Madison's religious beliefs. Certain historians claim to find reasons why Madison is believed to have had Deist influences on his thinking. Others say Madison had a Christian viewpoint and was led by it. He made the zealous proposal that the rising stars of his generation renounce their secular outlook and "publicly...declare their dissatisfaction by becoming fervent advocates of the cause of Christ." Two months later, Madison renounced his spiritual prospects and began studying law. The following year he entered the political arena, serving as a member of the Orange County Committee of Safety. Public service seems to have displaced earlier traces of faith from his consciousness. For the rest of his life there is no mention in his writings of Jesus Christ or any of the issues that might concern a practicing Christian. At the end of retirement there are a few cryptic references to religion, but nothing more.

Military Service and Early Political Career

After graduating from Princeton, Madison became interested in Britain's relationship with its American colonies, which continued to deteriorate over disagreements about British taxes. In 1774, Madison secured a seat on the local committee of safety, a pro-independence group that oversaw the militia. This first step into political life was facilitated by the privileged position his family maintained. In October 1775, he was commissioned a colonel in the Orange County militia, although he did not serve in combat for health reasons.

During the American Revolutionary War, Madison served in the Virginia state legislature (1776-1779) and became a protégé of Thomas Jefferson. He had previously seen the persecution of Baptist preachers in Virginia, who had been arrested for preaching without a license by the established Anglican church. Hence he collaborated with Baptist preacher Elijah Craig to promote the government's guarantee of the right to religious freedom in Virginia. These ideas about religious freedom affected James' way of thinking, influencing what he came to include in the U.S. Bill of Rights.

Madison gained prominence in Virginia politics by working with Thomas Jefferson in writing the *Virginia Statute for Religious Freedom* which was passed in 1786. The statute diminished the power of the Church of England and removed the power of the state in religious matters. It excluded Patrick Henry's plan to encourage citizens to give tax money to a church of their choice. In 1777, Madison's cousin, the Reverend James Madison, (1749-1812) became president of the College of William and Mary. Under the influence of Madison and Jefferson, Reverend Madison led the distancing of Britain and the Church of England.

As the youngest delegate to the Continental Congress, (1780-1783) Madison was considered a hard worker and someone who could easily form alliances. He persuaded the state of Virginia to relinquish its Northwest Territories, now owned by Ohio, to the Continental Congress. This completed the new Northwest Territory in 1783, a territory overseen by the federal government from which new states were formed. The territory claimed by the state of Virginia was in conflict with land claimed by the states of Connecticut, Pennsylvania, and Maryland. The latter states also ceded western territory to the federal government after agreeing that these lands would become new states. The Northwest Ordinance prohibited slavery in the territory north of the Ohio River, but did not outlaw the slavery that existed there because of the families already living in these territories.

Madison was once again elected to the Virginia House of Delegates to serve the 1784-1786 term during the early years of the new country. During this term, Madison became increasingly frustrated with what he called "excessive democracy." He criticized delegates for being more concerned with the local interests of their constituents, even if these interests were harmful to the state as a whole. He was particularly concerned about a law that denied diplomatic immunity to national ambassadors and another law that legalized paper money. He believed that delegates should be disinterested in local affairs and act only in the interest of the state, even if this directly contradicted what the constituents wanted. Madison believed that this "excessive democracy" was the cause of a social decay not seen before the beginning of the Revolution and which was reaching a tipping point (as exemplified by Shays' rebellion).

Father of the Constitution

The Articles of Confederation established the United States as an association of sovereign states with a weak central government. This deal was spurned and served little purpose after the Revolutionary War. Congress did not have the right to impose taxes and thus, could not pay the expenses it had incurred during the war, something that worried Madison and other nationalists such as George Washington and Alexander Hamilton, who feared the possibility of becoming disunited and bankrupt. Historian Gordon S. Wood has noted that many leaders, including Madison and Washington, were more fearful of the possibility that the revolution had not fixed the social problems that had created it in the first place, and that the excesses that had been blamed on Britain's king were being duplicated in state legislatures. Shays' rebellion is described as the event that forced a dialogue regarding the issue. Wood argues that many noted this event as the extreme effect of too much democracy.

As Madison writes, "a crisis has arrived in which it is to be decided whether the American experiment will be a blessing to the world, or whether the hopes which the republic had inspired will burst." Partly on Madison's initiative, a national assembly was called in 1787. Madison became key to George Washington's presence. He worked hard to convince him to attend because he knew how important he would be to the adoption of a new constitution. Years earlier, Madison had read book after book that Jefferson had sent him from France on various types of government. Historian Douglas Adair called this work of Madison's "probably the most fruitful scholarly research ever undertaken by an American." Many argue that this research prepared him for the convention. As he approached a quorum to begin the assembly, Madison, who was then 36 years old, wrote what became known as the Virginia plan, and the rest of the convention scrambled to amend the Virginia plan and complete it. Although the Virginia plan was more an outline of a constitution than a serious proposal, it was refined extensively, especially by John Rutledge and James Wilson on the committee of detail. Its use in the convention led many to call Madison the Father of the Constitution.

During the convention, Madison gave speeches more than 200 times. His co-delegates viewed him favorably. William Percy wrote, "Every person recognizes his greatness. In handling every big question, he took the lead in the convention. He always excels in being the best informed person in every debate." Madison wrote the minutes of the convention, writings that became the only comprehensive source of information on what happened during the meeting. Historian Clinton Rossiter considers Madison's performance a "combination of learning, experience, purpose, and imagination that not even Adams or Jefferson could match."

Gordon Wood argues that Madison's frustrating experiences in the Virginia legislature years earlier were part of the development of the ideas for the constitution. Wood notes that the governmental structure in the Virginia Plan and the final constitution were not innovative, as they were copied from the British government, had been used in the states since 1776, and numerous authors of the time had argued for their use at the national level. The controversial elements of the Virginia plan were not included and the rest were already considered necessary to successfully administer a government (state or national) decades earlier, hence Madison's contributions are considered more qualitative. Wood argues that like many contemporary politicians, Madison believed that the problem was not the Articles of Confederation, but the nature of a legislature. He believed that restraint of the states was needed, something that required more than altering the Articles of Confederation. It required a change of viewpoint regarding national union. The main question of the convention then would not be how to design a new government, but what sovereignty remained over the states, how much sovereignty should be transferred to the central government, or whether the constitution should end somewhere in the middle.

Those who like Madison believed that democracy in the state legislatures was too much and "insufficiently disinterested" wanted sovereignty transferred to the federal government, while others like Patrick Henry, who did not think this was a problem, thought only of fixing the articles of confederation. Madison was one of the few who intended to deprive the states of their sovereignty completely for the reason that this, to his way of thinking, was the only solution to the problem. Although there were many delegates who agreed with him, they at the same time disagreed with Madison on this, as it would be an extreme departure from the practice at the time. Although Madison lost many of the arguments he had in terms of fixing the Virginia plan, he gradually moved the debate away from those who argued for total state sovereignty. Since the question of the convention was to whom sovereignty belonged, Madison was very important to the final results. Wood notes that Madison's contributions came to be, not a design for a new type of government, but rather to answer the sovereignty question through a middle ground solution in which the states and the government share power.

The Federalist Papers and the Ratification Debates

After the Philadelphia convention there came to be intense debate regarding the ratification of the constitution. Each state was asked to take the constitution to their own legislatures to deliberate and vote for or against ratification. Madison became a leader in promoting ratification. For this purpose, Madison, Alexander Hamilton, and John Jay teamed up to write what became known as "*The Federalist Papers,*" a series of 85 newspaper articles to explain how the constitution would be implemented, primarily by way of countering the criticisms raised against the constitution by anti-Federalists.

These also came together for printing as a book, thus becoming just like a handbook for supporters of the constitution who would attend ratification conventions in their home states. Historian Clinton Rossiter called *The Federalist Papers* the most important work ever written by anyone in the past or future history of American political science. They were not impartial or scholarly arguments, but political arguments, written for the purpose of helping the New York Federalists, who were against the only coordinated movement in the country. One reason Madison was involved in writing the essays was because he was a member of the old-fashioned Confederate Congress, which would meet for the last time in New York.

If Virginia, the most populous state at the time, did not ratify the new constitution, it would not pass. When Virginia's ratification convention began on June 2, 1788, the constitution had not yet been approved by the required nine states. New York, the second most populous state and the most anti-Federal state, would certainly not ratify the constitution if Virginia did not. Moreover, if Virginia did not ratify the constitution, then it would not be part of the new union, something that would disqualify George Washington as a candidate for president of the new United States. The Virginia delegates were convinced that Washington's election was an implied term by agreeing to ratify the constitution and the new government. Many argue that the most popular person other than Washington was the powerful orator Patrick Henry, an anti-Federalist who was a delegate from Virginia (Washington was not a delegate). Most of the Virginia delegates believed that the people of their state did not agree with the proposed new government. At first, Madison did not intend to be elected to the Virginia convention, but ultimately had to take part as the situation seemed to indicate that ratification would not take place. By being part of the convention, Madison became a large part of the reason that the ratification of the constitution in Virginia, and thus the ratification of the constitution in general, was approved.

Since the states distrusted the central governments, ratifying the constitution was a difficult process. Patrick Henry thought the constitution would deny rights to the states and citizens. At the ratification convention in Virginia, Madison, who was a lousy speaker, had to argue publicly against Henry, who was the most important speaker in the country. Although Henry spoke in more dramatic and powerful tones, Madison successfully matched his performance. Henry's arguments were emotional arguments that left the audience with questions about undesirable future possibilities, while Madison's arguments answered their questions with reasonable answers. So great was the difference that Madison went so far as to call Henry's arguments absurd. Madison asserted that the new government would be a government with few and well-defined duties. Madison persuaded prominent figures such as Edmund Randolph, who had refused to accept the constitution at the Philadelphia convention, but came to accept it at the Virginia convention. Randolph's change of heart most likely convinced other delegates to support the constitution. When the time came to vote for the constitution, it appeared that it would be defeated, so Madison and a small group of Anti-Federalists begged them to vote for the constitution, promising that if it was accepted, he would see that a "Bill of Rights" was written and added to the constitution.

A resolution was proposed, to write a bill of rights for the consideration of the other states before ratifying the constitution. This found support in George Mason and Patrick Henry but was not supported by Madison, Henry Lee III, John Marshall, Randolph or Bushrod Washington. The resolution failed 88-80. Lee, Madison, Madison, Marshall, Randolph, and Washington then voted in favor of a resolution to ratify the new constitution, which was approved by the convention on June 28, 1789 on a vote of 89-79. Mason and Henry voted in the minority.

In terms of slavery and the constitution, Madison considered the Negro race to be an "unfortunate race" and believed that it was destined to be human property. On February 12, 1788, Madison in Federalist Essay No. 54. asserted that the Three-Fifths Compromise was the best alternative for the present condition of the slaves and for their representation as citizens in Congress. Madison believed that slaves would be protected by their masters and by the government.

Madison was called "Father of the Constitution" while he was alive. Modestly he responded to the title as "a credit to which I have no claim The Constitution was not, like the fabled goddess of wisdom, the offspring of a single brain. It must be considered the work of many minds and hands." He wrote Hamilton to the New York ratifying convention, stating his opinion that the "ratification was *in toto* and forever."

Member of Congress

Madison had been a delegate to the confederate congress, and wanted to be elected to the senate of the new congress in the new administration. The vindictive Patrick Henry was determined to deny him this seat, which is why he brought issue after issue to deliberation in the Confederate Congress in order to give Madison no chance to campaign. He also used his position to prevent the Virginia legislature from approving him as Virginia's senator either. When Madison then decided to run for election to the House of Representatives, Patrick redrew his district so that there would only be anti-Madison people in it, and thus he would lose any campaign he had run. Madison then decided that he would be elected to represent another district. Patrick then passed a new law requiring that every representative must live in the district he or she represented. After a time, this law was deemed unconstitutional but, at the time, it hindered Madison's career. Madison went on to run against James Monroe, another future president. The two campaigned together. Some time later, when Madison was already president, many of his constituents informed him that, had the weather not been bad on election day, he most likely would have lost the campaign. Madison defeated Monroe and later became a major leader in Congress.

Father of the Bill of Rights

Although the idea of a Bill of Rights had already been proposed during the Philadelphia convention, the delegates were anxious to return home, and thought the matter unnecessary. The lack of a bill of rights then became the most compelling argument the Anti-Federalists had. Although none of the colonies made a bill of rights a condition of ratification of the constitution, there were states that came close to doing so, something that would have prevented ratification. Some Anti-Federalists continued to argue about the absence of the bill of rights and even threatened to start over in a new constitutional convention. This new convention would most likely have been more divided than the first. Madison was against a bill of rights for multiple reasons. One of these was that the bill of rights was intended to protect citizens from the misuse of powers that the central government did not have in the first place, hence he thought it was unnecessary. He also thought that it was dangerous to have a bill of rights since the enumeration of certain rights of the citizen could be interpreted to mean that some right that was not written down would be a right that citizens did not have. There was also the possibility that, just as at the state level in some cases, even if it was written under the citizen's bill of rights, some state governments ignored the laws.

Although many in the new congress did not want to debate a possible bill of rights, (for the next century the bill of rights was considered the bill of rights and not the first 10 amendments to the constitution), Madison pressured congress to do so. congress was more concerned with fixing the new government and wanted to wait to see what defects came out before amending the constitution and the anti-federalists who would have supported the amendments promptly disbanded after the constitution was passed. And even if the Anti-Federalists were not trying to start over with a new convention, Madison feared that the states would urge their congressmen to do so, something the states had the right to do. Madison believed that the new constitution did not have the power to protect the national government from excessive democracy and localist mentality (the problem he kept noticing in state governments) and he thought a bill of rights might mitigate these problems. On June 8, 1789 Madison introduced the bill that would create amendments consisting of new articles in which 20 amendments were defined, depending on how one counted. Madison proposed primarily that the amendments be incorporated somewhere within the constitution. The house of representatives approved many of his amendments, but refused to incorporate them into the constitution, opting instead to write the amendments separately and tie them to the end of the constitution, thus sending it to the senate for approval.

The Senate agreed to edit the amendments further, making 26 changes and reducing the amendments to 12. Madison's proposal that the bill of rights apply to the federal government as well as the state government was dropped as was his editing of the preamble. A House-Senate conference then took place to settle the differences between the two proposals. On September 24, 1789, the committee finalized and produced a report of 12 amendments for consideration by the House and Senate. This final version was approved by the congress on September 25, 1789 by a joint resolution.

Articles 3 through 12 were ratified on December 15, 1791 and became the declaration of rights. Article 2 became the 27th amendment to the constitution and was ratified on May 7, 1792. The first article is still pending, awaiting approval by the states.

Foreign Policy Debates

When Britain and France went to war in 1793, the United States became caught in the middle. The 1778 Treaty of Alliance with France was still in effect, but most of the trade came from Britain. A second war with Britain seemed inevitable in 1794 when the British seized hundreds of ships trading with French ports. Madison thought Britain was weak and the United States was strong enough to wage a trade war, where ports would be ordered to deny trade with the British. This, although it would risk an actual war, if successful, would be a signal to the rest of the world of the independence and strength of the new United States. Historian Varg explains that Madison held the idea that "their interests may be mortally wounded, while ours are invulnerable."

The British West Indies, Madison said, could not survive without American food while the Americas did not need British food. However, Washington secured secure trade between the country and Britain through the Jay Treaty of 1794. Madison was very much against the treaty and by managing to mobilize popular support would result in the country's first political parties. Madison was defeated in the Senate and House of Representatives, which led to the next ten years of prosperity for the United States, but the enmity of the French. Since this was of great public interest, many people were divided and began to consider themselves either Federalist or Jeffersonian Republican.

Electoral History

1789

Madison was elected to the House of Representatives with 57.73% of the vote, defeating James Monroe.

1790

Madison was re-elected to the House of Representatives with 97.79% of the vote, defeating James Monroe.

Founding of the Democratic-Republican Party

Those who supported ratification of the constitution came to be known as the Federalist party. Those who did not support the constitution became known as the anti-federalist party, but neither group could be considered a political party in the modern sense. After the adoption of the new constitution and the new government in 1789, two political factions formed around the same arguments that were contested before. Those who supported Alexander Hamilton's attempts to aggrandize the national government were called Federalists, while those against him were called Republicans. (History calls the latter group the Democratic-Republican Party). Madison and other Democratic Party organizers, who favored states' rights and local control, struggled to find a solution to the institutional problem in the face of the Constitution's inability to prevent a concentration of power in a future Republican administration.

As the first secretary of the treasury, Hamilton created many new federal institutions, one of which included the First Bank of the United States. Madison led the unsuccessful attempt in Congress to block the creation of the bank, proposed by Alexander Hamilton. He argued that the constitution did not give the new government permission to create a central bank explicitly. On May 26, 1792, Hamilton complained "Mr. Madison, cooperating with Mr. Jefferson, are in command of the faction decidedly hostile to me and my administration." On May 5, 1792 Madison commented to Washington "With respect to the party spirit he was carrying on, I was sensible of its existence." Madison was elected to membership in the American Academy of Arts and Sciences in 1794.

In 1798 under President John Adams, the United States entered into a *de facto* war against France. The Quasi-War involved warships against commercial vessels in the Caribbean. The Federalists created an active army and supported laws against French refugees who became involved in American politics and against Republican editors. Congressman Madison and Vice President Jefferson, enraged, secretly wrote the Kentucky and Virginia Resolutions which declared the new Alien and Sedition Acts unconstitutional and noted that the "states, in opposing obnoxious laws, should interpose to arrest the progress of wickedness." These resolutions were not popular, as they assumed that the states had the right to invalidate federal laws. Jefferson went further by urging the states to secede if necessary, although Madison was able to convince Jefferson to change his extreme point of view.

According to historian Chernow, Madison's position "was an astonishing change of heart for a man who had pleaded at the Constitutional Convention for a national veto over state laws." Chernow feels that Madison's policy was aligned to Jefferson's positions until his experience as president with a weak national government in the War of 1812 caused Madison to appreciate the need for a strong central government to aid in national defense. At that same time he also began to support the idea of a national bank, a stronger navy, and an active army.

Historian Gordon S. Wood notes that Lance Banning, exemplified by what he wrote in his book *Sacred Fire of Liberty* (1995), "is the only modern historian who maintains the idea that Madison did not change his mind in the 1790s." In asserting this, Banning downplays Madison's nationalism in the 1780s. Wood concedes that many historians struggle to understand Madison, but Wood analyzes him as a man of his time- as a nationalist-but one with a different concept from the nationalism of the Federalists. He wanted to avoid a European-style government and was always convinced that the embargo against the French would have been successful. Hence Wood analyzes Madison from another point of view. Gary Rosen and Banning use other methods to analyze Madison's way of thinking.

Marriage and Family

Madison was 43 years old when he first married, which was considered very late at the time. On September 15, 1794, James Madison married Dolley Payne Todd, a 26-year-old widow, in Harewood, West Virginia, a place now known as Jefferson County. Madison never had children but did adopt Dolley's son from her first marriage, John Payne Todd, after the marriage.

Dolley Payne was born on May 20, 1768 in the Quaker-inhabited 'New Garden' settlement in North Carolina where her parents, John Payne and Mary Coles Payne, lived briefly. Dolley's sister, Lucy Payne, had recently married George Steptoe Washington, a relative of President Washington. As a member of Congress, Madison undoubtedly met the widow Todd at her social functions in Philadelphia, the nation's capital at the time. She had lived there with her deceased husband. In May 1794, Madison asked a mutual friend, Aaron Burr, to arrange an appointment with Dolley. In August, Dolley accepted her proposal of marriage. By marrying Madison, a non-Quaker bachelor, Dolley was expelled from her religion, the Society of Friends, which disapproved of marriage with members of other Christian denominations.

The two were known to maintain a happy marriage. Dolley Madison used her social skills when the two lived in Washington while James was secretary of state. When the White House was being built, Dolley advised on decorum and presiding at ceremonial functions for President Jefferson, a widower and friend of the two. When James became president, Dolley used her position as the president's wife to advance her husband's agenda, thus creating the position of first lady. Many consider her to be the reason James was so popular.

James' father died in 1801 at the age of 78. Madison inherited the large estate in Montpelier and other securities held, in addition to his father's 108 slaves. He had been managing the paternal estates since 1780.

Secretary of State (1801-09)

When Thomas Jefferson was inaugurated as president in 1801, he appointed him as his secretary of state. At the beginning of his term, Madison was a party to a supreme court case, *Marbury v. Madison* (1803) in which it was disputed how much power any judicial review would have, something that had upset Jefferson's supporters since they did not want a federal judicial branch with so much power. Jefferson had found it difficult to remain neutral during Napoleon's wars. During Jefferson's tenure, much of Europe was involved in some warfare beginning with France against Austria. After the Battle of Austerlitz in 1805 when the French decisively defeated the Austrian Habsburgs, the war then became a war between the United Kingdom and France.

Just before the beginning of Jefferson's presidency, Napoleon took control of the French directory, a department that had mismanaged the country's finances and was directly responsible for the loss of the army in its struggle to stop the slave rebellion in the colony of Saint-Domingue (Haiti). In 1802, Napoleon sent a troop of 20,000 men to the island to reestablish black slavery, as its sugar cane plantations had been the country's most important source of money. In addition to losing battles, the troops were also decimated by yellow fever. Seeing major losses in the New World, Napoleon saw no future in the West, which is why he sold the Louisiana Territory to Jefferson and Madison in 1803. Later that year, the 7000 troops remaining on the island were withdrawn and in 1804, Haiti declared its independence and became the second republic in the New World.

Many contemporaries, and later historians such as Ron Chernow, ignored his view that the constitution legalized only "strict construction" and thus took advantage of the opportunity to purchase the Louisiana Territory. Jefferson would have preferred to have had an amendment to the constitution authorizing the purchase, but aside from not having time, he noted that it was not required to do so. The Senate quickly ratified the treaty completing the purchase. Just as quickly, the House of Representatives also approved the purchase. With the Napoleonic wars still raging in Europe, Madison tried to keep the United States neutral and insisted on the country's rights under international law as applied to neutral states.

Even so, neither London nor Paris showed respect for the United States, which is why relations between the two countries deteriorated during Jefferson's second term. After his victory at Austerlitz over his enemies in continental Europe, Napoleon became more aggressive and ordered an embargo against the United Kingdom with the purpose of starving the British, something that ruined both countries. Madison and Jefferson decided to order an embargo against both countries, although the embargo was against all foreign countries. The embargo failed in the United States in the same way it failed in France by economically affecting ports all along the eastern seaboard, ports that depended on foreign trade. In the Northwest, the Federalists fought the embargo and thus found popularity among the American people. The embargo failed to be renewed just before the end of Jefferson's term.

Election of 1808

As Jefferson's second term was ending, his plans to retire became known, so the party began to promote the idea of electing Madison to the presidency in 1808. This was opposed by Representative John Randolph, who broke ties with Madison and Jefferson. The Democratic-Republican party's presidential clique was in charge of choosing the candidate and resolved to choose James Madison over James Monroe. Since the Federalist party had lost influence outside of New England, Madison easily defeated Federalist Charles Coteworth Pinckney.

Presidency (1809-17)

After his inauguration, Madison encountered immediate opposition in trying to appoint Albert Gallatin as secretary of state The leader of the opposition, William B. Giles, was able to force Madison to appoint Gallatin to the position of secretary of the treasury, a position he had held since Jefferson's previous presidency The talented Swiss Gallatin was Madison's chief advisor, political planner, and confidant. Madison appointed Robert Smith, the secretary of the navy, to the post of secretary of state. For the post of secretary of the navy, Madison appointed Paul Hamilton. Madison's cabinet, a group of people known to be of mediocre talent, was chosen for the purpose of appeasing the political opposition. When Madison became president in 1809, the federal government had a surplus of $9,500,000. By 1810, the national debt was down and taxes were reduced.

United States Bank

Madison intended to continue Jefferson's goals, particularly to undo the system and ideas left by previous Federalist presidents Washington and Adams. One of the pressing issues for Madison was the First Bank of the United States. The bank was to be funded until 1811. Although the secretary of finance urged the bank's existence, Congress was unable to reauthorize it. During the war against Great Britain, Congress realized that without a national bank, it was impossible to finance the army, so Congress passed a bill in 1814, authorizing a second national bank. Madison vetoed the bill. In 1816 Congress again passed a second national bank. This time it was approved by Madison having experienced the need for one.

Prelude to War

By 1809, the Federalist party lacked support apart from a few places in the north. Some long-time members such as John Quincy Adams, who now served as Madison's ambassador to Russia, had joined the Republican Party with Madison. Although it appeared that only one party was dominating American politics, the Republican party was divided and its future breakup would serve as the basis for the modern American political party system. Particularly as hostilities against Great Britain appeared to be inevitable, these factions took positions either for or against the war. The dominant faction was pro-war and was led by Speaker of the House Henry Clay. When the war finally broke out, it was led by Clay as well as Madison. This was by strategy, as Madison preferred the idea of checks and balances.

Napoleon had won a major battle, the Battle of Austerlitz in 1805, and as a result, Europe maintained peace for the next several years. Congress repealed Jefferson's embargo shortly before the beginning of Madison's term. The new U.S. trade policy was to continue trade with the United Kingdom and France only if these countries removed shipping restrictions. Madison's diplomatic efforts in April 1809 to convince the United Kingdom to cancel its trade war, although they had begun well, were rebuffed by British Foreign Secretary James Canning. By August 1809 diplomatic relations deteriorated further when Minister David Erskine was removed and replaced by "the hatchet man" Francis James Jackson. Madison resisted entering the war in opposition to the many calls to do so. In his 1795 political remarks, Madison wrote:

After Jackson accused Madison of duplicity with Erskine, Madison ordered Jackson removed from the state department and returned to Boston. During his first State of the Union address in November 1809, Madison asked Congress for its advice and alternatives concerning the trade crisis between the United States and Great Britain and warned about the possibility of war between the two countries. By the spring of 1810, Madison specifically asked Congress for more appropriations to increase the army and navy in anticipation of war. This, along with the effects of the peace Europe was enjoying, helped the U.S. economy grow. By the time Madison was preparing for reelection, the Spanish War of Independence was raging while, at the same time, Napoleon invaded Russia, and the European continent was again embroiled in hostilities.

The War of 1812

The United States went to war against the United Kingdom in 1812, a war that was, in many respects, part of the Napoleonic Wars. Napoleon began his Continental Blockade with the intent of forcing the other European countries to participate in his embargo against the United Kingdom. Although initially successful in starving the United Kingdom, Portugal refused to participate, which led to peninsular warfare. This, in turn, caused the Spanish colonies in South America to become neglected. Soon, the United Kingdom would be the most powerful force in the Atlantic.

As pressure against Napoleon increased, Britain also began to harass American ships. Some of the British tactics immediately infuriated the United States. Britain used its navy to prevent American trade with the French. The United States, in turn, saw this as a violation of international law. The British Royal Navy boarded U.S. ships while they were at sea to levitate their sailors, being in need of people to work on British ships. The United States considered this a transgression against U.S. sovereignty akin to a land invasion. Britain also armed Indian tribes in the Northwest Territories and encouraged them to attack the colonists even after ceding the territory to the United States in two separate treaties in 1783 and 1794.

Americans were calling for a "second war of independence" to restore the country's honor and power. The angry electorate voted for congressmen whose positions were pro-war such as Henry Clay and John C. Calhoun. Madison asked Congress for a declaration of war, which passed along party lines. The Federalists in the Northeast were intensely opposed to the war, having suffered economically from Jefferson's embargo against the French.

In haste, Madison asked Congress to put the country "in armor and in the attitude demanded by the crisis" by calling for the upgrading of the army, militia preparations, completion of the military academy, ammunition stockpiling, and expansion of the navy. Madison faced several challenges. His cabinet was divided, his political party fragmented, an unruly congress, obstructionist governors, incompetent generals, and militias that refused to fight outside their states. More serious than all was the lack of united support. There were serious threats of disunity in New England as they continued to smuggle contraband across the border into Canada and failed to provide finances for their soldiers. The problems were even more serious because Madison and Jefferson had worked to dismantle the system created by Hamilton and the Federalists. Both had reduced the size of the army, closed the U.S. bank, and tightened the tax system. They distrusted active armies, they distrusted banks, and dismantling the tax system meant that the government could not hire mercenaries. By the time the war began, Madison's military force consisted of poorly trained militias.

The higher command in the War Department proved to be either incompetent or cowardly. The general in Detroit surrendered to a small British force without firing a bullet. At the national treasury, Gallatin discovered that it would be impossible to finance the war, as the national bank was closed and bankers in the northeast refused to finance a war. Madison then contemplated invading Canada and seizing the territory and thus providing food coming from the West Indies, something that would be useful in negotiating peace. But all invasion efforts failed. The militias either decided not to fight the war or refused to leave their states. The British armed the Northwest Indians, notably several tribes allied with the Shawnee chief Tecumseh. But after losing control of Lake Erie in 1813, the British were forced out of the area. General William Henry Harrison caught up with them at the Battle of the Thames where he was able to destroy the British and Indian forces and also killed Tecumseh, a fact that demoralized the Indian forces in the Lake District permanently. Madison is the only president who commanded troops while still president even though he lost that Battle of Bladensburg. The British then invaded the city of Washington as Madison retreated with a disheartened militia. Madison's wife, Dolley, stayed behind and rescued certain valuable items from the White House, the Capitol, and other buildings, escaping just before the entry of the British.

By 1814, Andrew Jackson and William Henry Harrison destroyed all threats to the south and west respectively. As part of the war effort, a shipyard was built for the U.S. Navy at Sackets Harbor, New York, where thousands of men built twelve warships and had one more nearly completed by the end of the war. By the end of 1814, Madison and his Secretary of War James Monroe tried, unsuccessfully, to call up 40,000 men for forced service in the army. Anti-war Congressman Daniel Webster of New Hampshire strongly criticized the proposal, which is why it failed.

In a famous three-hour battle against HMS Java, HMS Constitution was nicknamed "Old Ironsides. The U.S. fleet engaged the British fleet in Lake Erie, although the British fleet was superior in numbers and capability. Even so, the U.S. fleet defeated the British fleet, capturing some ships and destroying the others. Commander Oliver Hazard Perry reported his victory with the simple phrase "We have met the enemy, and they are ours." The United States had built the largest merchant fleet in the world even though it had been reduced by Jefferson and Madison. Madison authorized certain ships to be privateers during the course of the war. Armed, they captured 1,800 British ships.

The courageous and successful defense of Fort McHenry, which defended the entrance to Baltimore Bay, against one of the heaviest bombardments in history (24 hours) inspired Francis Scott Key's poem "The Star Spangled Banner", a poem that served as the basis for the present U.S. national anthem. At New Orleans, General Andrew Jackson was able to assemble a force composed of American soldiers, members of the militia, frontiersmen, Creoles, Indians, and Jean Lafitte's pirates. The Battle of New Orleans took place for two weeks after the peace terms were written but not before their approval. The American defenders were able to hold off an invading British army and won the most important battle of the war. The Treaty of Ghent ended the war in February 1815, without any change of territory. Americans felt their honor had been restored in what became known as the "Second War of Independence." On March 3, 1815, the U.S. Congress authorized a campaign against Algiers and two squadrons of the navy were deployed in the region. The Second Barbary War would mark the definitive end of piracy in that region.

For most Americans, the fact that the burning of the capitol, the battle of New Orleans, and the treaty of Ghent happened in rapid succession left them with the impression that the battle of New Orleans forced the surrender of the British. This view, though incorrect, was the reason for the celebratory sentiment that lingered in the country for the next decade. It also helped explain the significance of the war even though it was strategically inconclusive. Napoleon was defeated for the last time at the Battle of Waterloo by the end of Madison's term, and as the Napoleonic Wars ended, so did the War of 1812. The last years of Madison's presidency were noted for the feeling of peace and prosperity, an era that came to be known as the "Era of Good Feelings." Madison's reputation also improved, and Americans finally felt they were part of a country with world power.

The Economy after the War and Internal Improvements

With peace finally established, Americans felt they had solidly secured independence from Great Britain. The Federalist party, which had called for the country's secession from the war at the Hartford Convention, was dissolved and disappeared from American politics. With Europe finally at peace, the era of good feelings described prosperity and a relatively even-handed political environment. Some political contentions lingered as, for example, in 1816, two-thirds of the representatives in the houses of congress lost their re-election on a vote for an increase in salary. Madison approved a national bank in the name of Alexander Hamilton, an effective system of taxation based on tariffs, a standing professional army, and other improvements promoted by Henry Clay under his American system. In 1816, retirement pensions were adjusted to include widows and orphans who were affected by the War of 1812 at half pay. Still, his last official action was a veto against a proposed law to improve streets, bridges, and canals.

Madison rejected the congressional view that the "General Welfare" provision of the Tax and Expenditure Cause justified the bill by saying:

Instead of this bill, Madison urged a variety of measures that he believed were "best executed under Federal authority" including general support for those canals and streets that would "further unite the several parts of our extended confederacy."

The Wilkinson Incident

James Wilkinson was a controversial American military commander, targeted to be governor of the Louisiana Territory by Thomas Jefferson in 1805. Wilkinson had been found involved in Aaron Burr's conspiracy to form a new nation in the west and take Spanish gold, but was exonerated in 1808. Jefferson decided to keep Wilkinson, a Republican, for political reasons.

When Madison became president in 1809, he appointed Wilkinson in charge of St. Bernard Parish on the Louisiana coast to protect the United States from a possible invasion. Wilkinson proved to be an incompetent general; many soldiers complained of his ineffectiveness: their tents were in disrepair and many fell ill with malaria, dysentery, and scurvy; dozens died daily.Wilkinson made excuses and refused to move troops further inland, away from the mosquito-infested swampy coast. A two-year congressional investigation was inconclusive, so the decision to keep or fire him came down to Madison. Like Jefferson, Madison decided to keep him for political reasons, as Wilkinson had influence over Republicans in northern Pennsylvania.

By retaining Wilkinson, Madison and Jefferson distinguished themselves by supporting army leaders for political reasons rather than competence. Historian Robert Allan Rutland describes how the incident scarred the reputation of the war department and left Madison surrounded by incompetent senior army members for the start of the War of 1812. Losing two battles against the British, Madison eventually dismissed Wilkinson from active military service.

Indians Insurance

At the beginning of his term in office on March 4, 1809, James Madison, in his first inaugural address, stated that it was the responsibility of the federal government to convert the American Indians by "their participation in the improvements of which the human mind and manners behave in a civilized state." Like Jefferson, Madison had a paternalistic view toward the American Indians, commending them toward agriculture. Although there are few details, Madison often hung out with southeastern and western tribes such as the Creek and Osage. Seeing pioneers and settlers moving further west and taking large territories from the Cherokee, Choctaw, Creek, and Chickasaw Indians, Madison ordered the U.S. Army to protect the Indians' lands, thus provoking the displeasure of his commander Andrew Jackson. Jackson insisted the president ignore the Indians' pleas to stop the invasion of their lands and resisted the president's orders. In the Northwest Territory after the Battle of Tippecanoe in 1811, the Indians lost their lands to Anglo settlers. By 1815, with a population of 400,000 Anglos, Indian land rights in Ohio were effectively declared null and void.

Administration and Cabinet

- Madison is the only president to see the deaths of two of his vice presidents while he was still president.

Judicial Notes

Supreme Court

Circuit Breaks

District Courts

States Admitted to the Union

- Louisiana - April 30, 1812.
- Indiana - December 11, 1816.

After the Presidency

When Madison finished his term of office in 1817, he retired to Montpelier, his tobacco estate in Orange County (Virginia) near Jefferson's Monticello estate. He was 65 years old. Dolley, who thought he would now have time to travel to Paris, was 49. Like Washington and Jefferson, Madison retired from the presidency financially poorer than when he began because of the low price of tobacco and the gradual financial collapse of his estate, due to poor management by his stepson.

A glimpse into Madison is provided by the first written White House biographical notes *A Colored Man's Reminiscences of James Madison* (1865), written by former Madison slave Paul Jennings who worked for the president from the age of 10, serving as a footman, and then as his valet for the rest of Madison's life. After Madison's death, Jennings was purchased in 1845 from Dolley Madison by Daniel Webster, who required him to work for pay and then acquire his freedom. Jennings published his short story in 1865. He had great respect for Madison and related how Madison never beat a slave, nor did he allow overseers to beat them as well. Jennings recounts that if any slave misbehaved, Madison would meet with him privately and they would discuss his behavior.

Some historians imagine that Madison's mounting debts are the main reason he kept his Philadelphia convention notes, and other important records he owned, secret and chose not to publish during his lifetime. "He knew the value of these notes and wanted them to add value to his will for Dolley's use in failing his estate. He expected $100,000 from the sale of his papers of which his notes were the gem." Madison's financial problems weighed on him and deteriorated his mental and physical health as they plagued him.

In his later years, Madison became extremely concerned with his historical legacy. He began to alter letters and other documents in his possession. He changed days and dates, adding and deleting words and phrases and altering handwriting. By the time he was in his seventies, his "clarifications" had become an obsession. As an example, he changed a letter he had written to Jefferson in which he criticized Lafayette; not only did he cross out entire passages, but he also copied Jefferson's handwriting style in writing his changes

In 1826, after Jefferson's death, Madison was appointed the second chancellor of the University of Virginia. He retained the position of chancellor of the college for ten years, until his death in 1836.

In 1829, at the age of 78, Madison was chosen as a representative to the constitutional convention in Richmond for the revision of the Virginia constitution. It was his last appearance as a legislator and constitutional writer. The issue of major importance at this convention was that of proportioning, the legal process by which representation is chosen from places and factions within the state. Districts in western Virginia complained that they were underrepresented because the state constitution provided voting districts by county rather than by population. Growing population increases in Piedmont and other western parts of the state were not reflected in legislative representation. Western reformers also wanted to extend the right to vote to all white men, rather than just landowners. Madison tried to find a compromise without success. Voting rights were finally extended to landowners and landlords, but eastern farmers refused to approve of proportioning on the basis of population. Madison was disappointed to see the failure of Virginians to find an equitable resolution to their problems.

Madison was concerned about the continuation of slavery in Virginia and the South in general. He believed that the best solution to slavery would be to return black people back to Africa when they regained their freedom, as promoted by the American Colonization Society. He told Lafayette at the time of the convention that colonization would create a "speedy effacement of this blot on our republican character." British sociologist Harriet Martineau visited Madison during his tour of the United States in 1834. She characterized his belief in colonization as a solution to slavery as "strange and incongruous." Madison, it is believed, sold or donated his Grain Mill to support the ACS. Historian Drew R. McCoy believes that "The Convention of 1829, we would say, pushed Madison to the brink of delirium, if not despair. The slavery dilemma undid him." Like most African Americans of the time, Madison's slaves wanted to stay in the United States, where they were born, and believed that their labor earned them citizenship. They resisted "repatriation".

Despite his deteriorating health, Madison wrote several political memoranda, including an essay against the appointment of chaplains to Congress and the armed forces. Although he agreed with the religious exclusion it would create, he knew it would not produce political harmony.

Between 1834 and 1835, Madison sold 25% of his slaves to recoup the financial losses of his estate. Madison lived until 1836 being ignored by American politics more and more. He died in Montpelier on June 28 as the last of the Founding Fathers of the United States He was buried in the Madison family cemetery in Montpelier.

In 1842, Dolley Madison sold the Montpelier mansion, and in 1844 he sold the extended estate to Henry W. Moncure. He rented half of the slaves to Moncure. The other half he bequeathed to his son John Payne Todd and James Madison Jr. a nephew. Between 1845 and 1849 Todd sold several of the slaves; by 1851 he was keeping only 15 at his residence. By 1850, the Montpelier estate was nothing more than a shadow of its former self. In 1851, Montpelier became the property of Thomas Thorton, an English gentleman. He owned 40 slaves.

The question of Freemasonry

William R. Denslow seems to have found evidence suggesting that James Madison may have been a Mason through a letter to Madison from John Francis Mercer in which he writes, "I have not had occasion before to congratulate you on your becoming a Mason- a very ancient and honorable fraternity." Yet, in an 1832 letter to Stephen Bates, James Madison appears to have written that he was never a Mason and that he was a "stranger to [his] principles."

Legacy

Historian Garry Wills wrote:

George F. Will once wrote that "if we truly believe that the pen is mightier than the sword, our nation's capital would have been named "Madison D.C. instead of Washington D.C."

Madison's writings are studied for debates about human rights among different classes of citizens in the twenty-first century. Madison seems to have anticipated the danger of a strong majority over a weak minority through the popular vote. Madison, in The Federelarists Papers, in Federalist No. 51, wrote:

In 1986, Congress created the *James Madison Memorial Fellowship Foundation as part* of the bicentennial celebration of the Constitution. The foundation provides $24,000 in college scholarships for high school teachers to earn their master's degree in constitutional studies. Montpelier, his family's estate, has been preserved as a National Historic Landmark.

Many counties, several towns, cities, educational institutions, a mountain range, and a river have been named in Madison's honor.